YOUR KNOWLEDGE HAS VALUE

AF131181

- We will publish your bachelor's and master's thesis, essays and papers

- Your own eBook and book - sold worldwide in all relevant shops

- Earn money with each sale

Upload your text at www.GRIN.com and publish for free

Bibliographic information published by the German National Library:

The German National Library lists this publication in the National Bibliography; detailed bibliographic data are available on the Internet at http://dnb.dnb.de .

Imprint:

Copyright © 2017 GRIN Verlag, Open Publishing GmbH
Print and binding: Books on Demand GmbH, Norderstedt Germany
ISBN: 9783668489837

This book at GRIN:

http://www.grin.com/en/e-book/366707/productions-and-service-operations-management

Mike G.

Productions and Service Operations Management

A Compact Overview

GRIN Publishing

GRIN - Your knowledge has value

Since its foundation in 1998, GRIN has specialized in publishing academic texts by students, college teachers and other academics as e-book and printed book. The website www.grin.com is an ideal platform for presenting term papers, final papers, scientific essays, dissertations and specialist books.

Visit us on the internet:

http://www.grin.com/

http://www.facebook.com/grincom

http://www.twitter.com/grin_com

Productions and Service Operations Management

To determine the optimal facility layout for any kind of company is a very tough task the operations manager (or founder him-/herself) has to tackle. However such tasks base on the same assumptions and functioning, a whole academic discipline arose since its importance was recognized in the late 1980s. Questions like the optimal decision making process, capacity considerations, scale effects or the best facility location between other production centers and the distributions centers within (bigger) cities are covered in this text. Especially for those who are interested in founding their own business, this text can be very helpful and interesting. It isn't only about the layout for steel companies, even modern service providers have to follow an optimal layout, called job shop, which can be optimized in the most cases. Many examples, images & figures as well as step-by-step calculations are performed to enable even "math strangers" to follow and align them to their own individual situation.

Starting with the Basics.

- **Goals of Operations Management.**
  - ○ Design, operations and improvements, not only for manufacturing, but also for service provision.
  - ○ Even though Marketing, Finance (incl. Accounting) and Operation are equally important, a whole business can't succeed over a longer period of time if their operating processes aren't efficient.
    - → Stronger focus on OM related to global competition.

- **Conversion Subsystem.**
  - ○ The "black box" of production, process of turning input into output.
    - ▪ Input are resources like personnel, equipment, raw material, semi-finished goods and information.
    - ▪ Outputs could be products or services.
  - ○ **5 P's of Operations Management are**
    - ▪ People (workforce).
    - ▪ Plants (focus on production or on sales).
    - ▪ Process.
    - ▪ Parts (raw-material, semi-finished or already finished goods).
    - ▪ Planing and control system (keep the processes at their top of efficiency).
  - ○ The future demand is considered to coordinate the needed flow of goods, services or information.
    - ▪ Forecast demand will allow the production planning.
    - ▪ After dealing with the procurement of the needed goods, the capacities and people have to be scheduled to ensure operate efficiency when implementing the production program.
  - ○ Perfect planing allows a seamless transition through this procedure.
    - → In reality many uncertainty occur and lead to several delays.
  - ○ Due to events which can't be forecasted, **inventory management** becomes more and more important → Provides security in uncertain times.

- **Types of Resources.**
  - ○ Human Resources like knowledge, skill and motivation of the workers.
  - ○ External immaterial resources like brand value or company's perception in the public.
  - ○ **Internal immaterial resources** could be the systems and processes.
  - ○ **Physical Resources** are facilities, cash and premises.
  - ○ Those resources determine the company's competences.
    - → In this lecture we will only focus on the last two kinds of resources.

- **Hierarchical Structure.**
  - ○ The company should be threaten as a whole even though it's hierarchy.
  - ○ **Strategic Management** is at the top and sets long-term strategies and goal for the firm.
    - ▪ Task is to plan the resources in general, made decisions influence the whole company.
  - ○ **Tactical Management** is constraint by the decisions of the strategic management.
    - ▪ Mostly consists of routine tasks, has to manage the resources to fulfill the plan from above.
    - ▪ Will work out production plans for each production facility.

- **Operations Management** is constraint by the decisions the tactical management made.
  - Task is to ensure the daily workflow and system performance.
  - Has to implement the production plan as (cost) efficient as possible.
- **The conceptional framework of these hierarchy.**
  - The flow of information is determined by the hierarchy.
    - Strategic Management will provide relevant information for the tactical management and operational management.

- Design of product, potential and process are streamlined processes.
  - The lower the stage in the hierarchy, the more detailed the tasks.

- **Apple Case.**
  - **Reduction of the product family.**
    - Only shared components and common technology.
  - **Focus on key features.**
    - They can meet the deadline, each year a new innovation.
  - **Inventory Management.**
    - From 70 days (500m $) to 30 days inventory turnover (end products).
    - Used their own management systems to optimize the process.
  - **Parts.**
    - Only remain 1 day in inventory.
    - Extremely efficient, best in the industry.
  - **Suppliers.**
    - Apple focuses on key features and outsource everything else.
    - Apple has market power to squeeze the suppliers.
      - Ensure quality, reduce costs, keep timeliness up.
    - 75% reduction in total number if suppliers.
  - **Warehouse.**
    - Total amount of warehouses was reduced by 50%.
  - **Delivery.**
    - Only 5% of the orders could be met at the same day initially.
    - Not over 75% of all offline and online orders can be met each day.
    => Summarize the strategy of Apple: Simplicity.

- **3 Major Fields in OM.**
  - Strategic Management deals with capacity planning (in general) and facility location.
  - Tactical Management deals with layout planning and production planning.
  - Operational Management deals with inventory management and capacity planning (s.str.).

- **Overview of Strategic Management Problems.**
  - ○ Decisions made at the top of the hierarchy regarding the whole company and considering multiple targets.
  - ○ Long-term significance on operational performance.
  - ○ Dealing with great uncertainties (many forecasts, e.g. political stability).
    - → Interaction with the environment to increase certainty.
    - => Fully consideration of all interdependencies between business areas need huge amount of managers time and capital.

- **Life Cycle Concept[1].**
  - ○ Period of time related to production of a certain product type.

Introduction phase	Developing (research & technology)	(huge) losses
Growth phase	Production is expanding (RTS)	Increasing profits
Maturity phase	Efficiency (redefine the production plan)	Maximum profits
Declining base	Product becomes obsolete (sale of machinery, licenses etc.)	Only few profits

Product Life Cycle

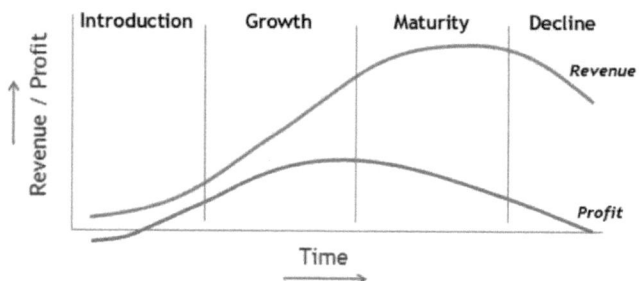

- **Concept of Capacity.**
  - ○ Capacity = potential of an economical unit in one period.
  - ○ Capacity design = generate expected goods or services as cost-efficient as possible.
  - ○ Trade-off between quantitative and qualitative capacity.
  - ○ Capacity is a relative term, can either be input or output.
  - ○ Capacity is constraint by bottlenecks (= shortages) // scarcity constraints.
    - ▪ Inadequate capacity, leads to longer waiting time for customers, potential for competitors.
  - ○ Capacity occupation is the opposite of a bottleneck.
    - ▪ Producing exceeds market demand, marketing has to generate artificial demand.
    - ▪ Prices has to be lowered to prevent future costs (storage, recycling, etc.).
  - ○ **Major concerns** of management regarding capacity management.

Vice president	Aggregate capacity	Financial resources available for the company	

1   Image Source: http://www.mrdashboard.com/images/Product_Life_Cycle.png

| Plant manager | Concrete capacity in one facility | Balance demand and supply | Shift production in advance to be secured for seasonal changes |
| First level superior | Optimal capacity to ensure daily workflow | Employee vacancy, overtime, hiring | |

=> Multiple problems have to be solved.
- Business strategy has to be competitive and must align with the corporate vision.

- **Kinds of Capacity Considerations.**
  - ○ **Capacity Expansion.**
    - Investment decision to expand capacity.
    - Will lead to huge costs, so therefore be sure that demand increase is long-term trend.
    - Short-term increases of demand could be handled by adjustments like overtime.
    - Medium-term increase demand can be handled with procurement.
      => Only if demand increase is sustainable, then invest in additional capacities.
  - ○ **Capacity Restructuring.**
    - Potential reasons for a capacity restructuring are
      - **Shift of demand**: Production must shift too
      - **Environmental regulations**: Facilities are no longer able to produce // restructuring is not feasible (reputation concerns).
      - **Technical Advancement**: Only products /machinery become obsolete and have to be renewed.
  - ○ **Capacity Return (Decrease).**
    - Disinvestment in machinery and layoff of employees.
    - Reduction of fixed costs, but reputation concerns and limited market for machinery (high recycle costs).

- **How to set up a decision tree.**
  - ○ Generic structure.
  - ○ *Given information.*
    - Planing horizon T = 2 years.
    - Investor faces the following payoffs {65, -10, 90}.
    - Debt interest rate s = 12%.
    - Deposit interest rate h = 6%.
    - Actions and related costs :

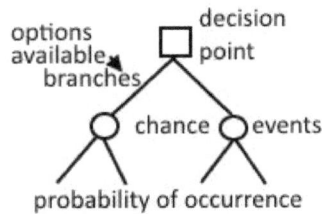

Action	Costs	
	$t = 0$	$t = 1$
Small Expansion	50	
Big Expansion	90	
Additional small expansion		25
Reduction of big expansion		-20
No action		0

- Profits per demand situation and probability of occurrence.

Demand	Capacity		Demand in 1st period	Demand in 2nd period
	low	high	low $P(L) = 60\%$	low $P(L|L) = 50\%$
low	50	50		high $P(H|L) = 50\%$
high	50	100	high $P(H) = 40\%$	low $P(L|H) = 20\%$
				high $P(H|H) = 80\%$

- (1) Set up the scenario analysis (which demand situation will occur).
- (2) Set up a static planning by assuming certainty.
  - Consider all possible actions of the investor.

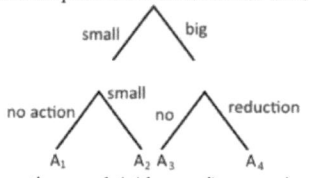

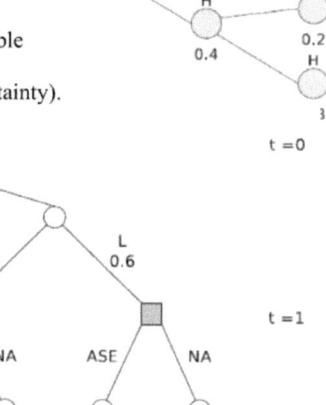

- 4 Alternatives and 4 (demand) scenarios imply 16 possible actions.
- (3) Set up the probability decision tree (because of uncertainty).

- (4) Calculate the related payoffs per action.
  - Example calculation for A_3S_2
  - Capital value in period 0: $CV_0 = 65 - 90 = -25$
    - Invest 90 in big investment and receive 65 for sure.
  - $CV_1 = (-10 + 0 + 50) + (-25 * 1.12) = 12$.
    - Receiving -10 in profits for sure, 0 because we don't do any further investment and 50 is the profit of our previous investment.
    - Right term is the loss form the last year with the respective time value.
  - $CV_2 = 90 + 100 + 12 * 1.06 = 202.72$
    - 90 in profits for sure, 100 though the investment from period 0 and 12 in profits from last year, included the time value of money.

- **Solution for all actions.**

	S_1	S_2	S_3	S_4	ECV
A_1	199.25	199.25	199.25	199.25	199.25
A_2	172.754	222.754	172.754	222.754	203.754
A_3	152.72	202.72	205.72	255.72	204.92*
A_4	173.92	173.92	226.92	226.92	195.12

- ○ (5) Calculate the expected cash value for each alternative (weighted average).
  - **ECV for alternative 2**: 172.754 * 0.3 (Prob for Low Low) + 222.754 * 0.3 (Prob for Low High) + 172.754 * 0.08 (Prob for High Low) + 222.754 * 0.32 (Prob for High High) = 203.754.
- ○ (6) Evaluate the best alternative by relating the highest expected capital value with the alternatives from the static setting (assumed no uncertainty).

- **Learning Curves.**
  - ○ Adding more products to one product line is more efficient due to learning effects.
    - Workers know approximately what to do, machines are already calibrated etc.
      - → Increase in overall efficiency due to existing (and constantly increasing) experience.
      - => Overall production costs and time will decrease.
  - ○ Learning process takes part over time (dynamic).
    - Qualitative and quantitative productivity will increase.
    - Enables to perform more (new) tasks.
      - → Hard to quantify and to relate to one single department.
        - Maybe able to assign learning effects only to the production department, but then the effects of the other departments leading to this learning are still within this learning effects.
      - => The more complex the task, the higher the learning effects.

- **Differentiation of Scale Effects.**

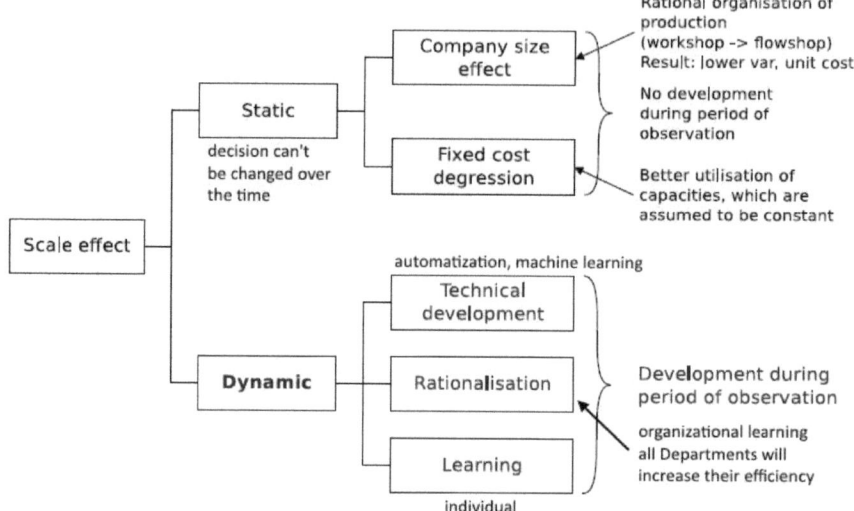

○ Static decisions can't be changed over time and will lead to fixed cost degression and company size effects (RTS).
○ Dynamic decisions enable to change the capacity planning after some time.
  ▪ Leads to learning effects for individuals (workers), machines (automatization) and the whole organization (all departments will benefit from this).

- **Experience Curve.**
  ○ Learning curve is production specific, experience curve is generalized.
  ○ Overall costs of the company are considered and related to cumulated production quantity.
    => Average value including quantitative and qualitative effects.
  ○ First verified by the electrical and chemical industry and first implemented in the airplane industry.
  ○ The higher the quantity produced, the lower the marginal and average costs.
  ○ But potential of cost reduction becomes smaller over the time until the point of **diseconomies of scale** is reached and overall costs increase again.
    → When the slope is constant, the learning effect is fully utilized.
  ○ **Numerical Example.**

Quantity produced	MC of last unit
1	100.000
2	80.000
4	64.000
8	51.200

double — 80% → 80% learning effect = 20% production rate
double → 80.000 * 0,8
double → 64.000 * 0,8

=> No reduction until 0, only until diseconomies of scale are reached
  ○ Always doublings of production quantity are considered.
  ○ Overall formula for experience curve $k_{(x)} = k_1 * X^{-b}$.

With k_1 = costs of first unit.
B = Degression factor
X = Cumulated production quantity
$k_{(x)}$ = costs of last unit

8

- **Relation between the learning effect and experience curve.**
  - Learning effect compares the costs of X units with 2*X units which will reveal a result of 2^{-b}
    - → Solving for b will give us all data needed for the experience curve.
  - $b = -\dfrac{\ln(q)}{\ln(2)}$ with $q = $ *learning effect* .

- **Turn Experience Curve into a Linear Degression.**
  - **Linearization.**
    - Formula for experience curves $k_{(x)} = k_1 * X^{-b}$ can be linearized by ln.
    - $\ln(k_{(x)}) = \ln(k_1) - b * \ln(X)$ and with simple substitution $\ln(k_{(x)}) = \overset{\circ}{k}_{(x)}$ leads to
    - $\overset{\circ}{k}_{(x)} = \overset{\circ}{k}_1 - b * \overset{\circ}{X}$ what can be solved by linear regression.
  - **How to estimate the different parameters.**

$$\hat{b} = \dfrac{n \cdot \sum\limits_{i=1}^{n}(x_i \cdot y_i) - \sum\limits_{i=1}^{n} x_i \cdot \sum\limits_{i=1}^{n} y_i}{n \cdot \sum\limits_{i=1}^{n} x_i^2 - \left(\sum\limits_{i=1}^{n} x_i\right)^2}$$

$$\hat{a} = \dfrac{\sum\limits_{i=1}^{n} y_i \cdot \sum\limits_{i=1}^{n} x_i^2 - \sum\limits_{i=1}^{n}(y_i \cdot x_i) \cdot \sum\limits_{i=1}^{n} x_i}{n \cdot \sum\limits_{i=1}^{n} x_i^2 - \left(\sum\limits_{i=1}^{n} x_i\right)^2}$$

  - **Practical Application.**
    - Following data are given.

iteration		real data = y			= x²	= x * y
i	x	$k(x)$	$\ln x$	$\ln k(x)$	$[\ln x]^2$	$\ln x \cdot \ln k(x)$
1	1	78	0	4.3567		
2	2	64	0.6931	4.1589		
3	4	47	1.3863	3.8501		
4	8	42	2.0794	3.7377		
5	16	41	2.7725	3.7136		
6	32	31	3.4567	3.4340		
7	64	26	4.1589	3.2581		
8	128	22	4.8520	3.1410		
9	256	20	5.5452	2.9957	30.7490	16.6119
10	512	17	6.2383	2.8332		
Sum			31.1916	35.4291	136.9291	101.0242

  - (1) Calculate $\hat{b}$ with the formula and data from above.
    $\hat{b} = \dfrac{10*101.0242 - 31.1916*35.4291}{10*16.9291 - (31.1916)^2} = 0.2392$.
  - (2) Calculate $\hat{k}_1$.
    $\hat{k}_1 = \dfrac{35.4291*16.9291 - 101.0242*31.1916}{10*16.9291 - (31.1916)^2} = 4.28292$.
  - (3) Undo the linearization for $\hat{k}_1$.
    $k_1 = e^{\hat{k}_1} = e^{4.28292} = 72.9147$.
  - (4) Set up the linear regression equation → Experience curve.
    $k_{(x)} = 72.9147 * X^{-0.2392}$.

9

- (5) Additionally the deviation can be calculated or illustrated.

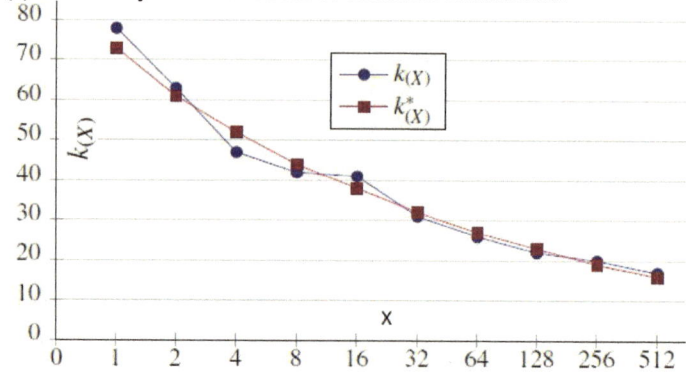

$\rightarrow$ The higher the quantity, the more precise the linear regression model.

- **Evaluation of the Experience Curve**.
  - (1) No separation of quantitative and qualitative effects.
    - $\rightarrow$ No detailed information provided.
  - (2) Not applicable to individual Departments (e.g. to identify negative learning effects) because its only the average.
  - (3) First unit k_1 is already influenced by experience from other product lines and therefore will mislead the whole regression analysis.
  - (4) Risk of overcapacity is not taken into account, if all companies follow the strategy of dual advantage, then excess supply will arise and prices have to be lowered to increase demand.
    - **Dual advantage strategy**: Combination of dynamic and static capacity planing leads to fixed cost degression and more experience.
  - (5) Possible conflicts between pure quantity and other policies like just in time production.
    - Larger quantities will decrease production costs, but increase storage costs.
    - Just in time production will increase production costs (due to non-optimal machine occupation) but minimize inventory costs.
      - $\rightarrow$ Inventory costs determine around 25% of total costs, so maybe JIT is cheaper.
    - $\Rightarrow$ Application of linear regression analysis is simple, but sometimes misleading.

- **Facility Location Decision**.
  - Companies have production (plants) and distribution (stores) facilities.
  - Normally distribution facilities have to be placed near the customers, e.g. in big cities.
  - Production facilities should be placed near the distribution ones to minimize transportation costs, but have the potential to reduce costs arising e.g. by taxes.
    - $\Rightarrow$ Facility location determined the relation between enterprise and environment.
  - **Optimal facility location**.
    - Determine primary and secondary goals.
    - Maximize the implementation of primary goals, but also try to implement as much of the secondary goals as possible.

Kind of facility	Primary goals	Secondary goals

Retailing / Sales	Close to the customers	Low transportation costs
Government facility	Close to citizens	Close to sub-facilities
Hospitals	Minimize response time	Overall cost reduction

- **When to make location decisions.**
  - Business foundation.
  - Company mergers.
  - Location changes due to cheaper production, lower wages, less regulations etc.
  - Alternatives of location changes are: partially shut down / expand or totally shut down / open another facility → Expansion of a current location is the cheapest way.
  - Exception: **Cloud manufacturing**; it has no business office, operates solely throughout the web.

- **Aspects of Location Planning.**
  - **Purpose of Location.**
  - **Determine the Location.**
    - Distinguish between macro and micro location.
      - **Macro location**: National or international location? Take into consideration: Overall law, political stability, currency exchanges.
      - **Micro location**: Region → Community → Side.
        - Region criteria: Availability of labor, infrastructure.
        - Community criteria: Real estates, subventions, tax conditions.
  - **Capacity Distribution.**
    - Especially really important in case of multiple facility locations.
    - Procurement and near to distribution centers is very important.
      - Load and distance will influence transportation costs. => Within the EU transportation costs make 9-20% of overall costs.
    - Question: How to determine where to locate a facility?
      - Find out the most attractive locations regarding local specifications and then determine which location (or how many of them) will minimize transportation costs.
  - **Market Segmentation.**

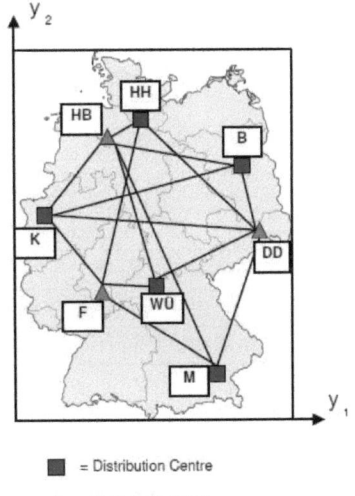

- **Multiple Location Problem – not in the Exam.**
  - If location planning was performed and several possible facilities are analyzed, it has to be determined which and how much of them should be opened to minimize the total costs (fixed costs of facility operations and transportation costs to distribution centers).
  - Use the Solver in Excel to find out the correct value.

■ = Distribution Centre

▲ = Potential Locations

$$Z = \underbrace{\sum_{i=1}^{I} f_i \cdot y_i}_{\text{total fixed costs}} + \underbrace{\sum_{i=1}^{I}\sum_{j=1}^{J} c_{ij} \cdot x_{ij}}_{\text{total transportation costs}} \rightarrow \min!$$

subject to:

I demand has to be satisfied
$$\sum_{i=1}^{I} x_{ij} = d_j \qquad j = 1,2,\dots,J$$

J capacity constraint, quantity in distribution
centers at least equal the transported quantity
$$\sum_{j=1}^{J} x_{ij} \le b_i \cdot y_i \qquad i = 1,2,\dots,I$$

$$x_{ij} \ge 0 \qquad \begin{array}{l} i = 1,2,\dots,I \\ j = 1,2,\dots,J \end{array}$$

non-negativity

binary variable
$$y_i \in \{0,1\} \qquad i = 1,2,\dots,I$$

Variables:

x_{ij} Transport quantity from location i to centre j

$y_i \begin{cases} 1, \text{ if location } i \text{ is chosen} \\ 0, \text{ else} \end{cases}$

Data:

d_j Demand of centre j

b_i Production capacity of location i

f_i Fixed costs of location i

c_{ij} Transport cost between location i and centre j

Indices:

i Index for potential locations

j Index for distribution centres

○ Location Planning will reveal the fixed costs and capacity of each possible facility.
○ Demand of each distribution center is already known by historical observation, set op transportation costs is also given.

Distribution Centres		Potential Locations		
Site	Demand	Site	Capacity	Fixed Costs
Würzburg	200	Dresden	400	60000
Berlin	250	Bremen	350	60000
Munich	150	Frankfurt	600	80000
Cologne	300			
Hamburg	100			

Transport Costs between Location i and Centre j					
Site	Würzburg	Berlin	Munich	Cologne	Hamburg
Dresden	270	170	400	450	300
Bremen	320	280	490	230	120
Frankfurt	120	390	240	230	370

○ By using the solver (for guideline see appendix) the following solution is revealed.
○ System is called **mixed integer program.**
  ▪ Only integers are allowed otherwise to many solutions are possible and problem becomes to complex to solve.
  ▪ Mixing integers and binaries.
  ▪ Abstract way to illustrate a decision problem.

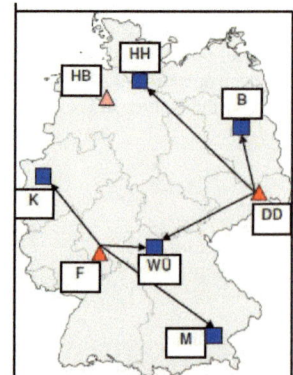

- **Tactical Management.**
  - Operate optimally under the constraints the strategic management set up.
  - Determining the inside of each facility; design and origin of machinery, workstations, departments, but also of „unimportant" decisions like kitchen and restrooms can be very important regarding efficiency.
  - **Two different kinds**: product layout design and process layout design.
    - Layout planning is the natural extension of production planning.
  - **Hierarchy of decisions.**
    - *Products or mixture of product families.*
      - Reflected in corporate mission / company strategy, determined by target customers.
    - *How to produce this products* (trade-off between flexibility and cost reduction).
    - *Determine the production process* (main characteristics are given by the previous consideration).
    - *Implement the production system* (= core of operations management).
      - Will balance demand and supply and optimize the production.
      => Continuous flow of information between production and layout process is required.

- **Layout Process.**
  - Starting with an empty floor the flow of personnel and machinery should be optimized to reduce delays and costs in general.
    - Inventory, machinery, workstations, restrooms etc. have to be arranged.
  - **Example for good layout process**: Googles facilities.
    - Target was to invest $ 3b into the office in Silicon Valley, but in the end it was about $ 5b.
    - Highly personalized offices, common rooms, kitchens; overall very comfortable.
    - → Should take away the pressure and stress related to the work at Google.
    - Infrastructure will be used for at least the next 30 years, so it should be suitable and sustainable.
    - Every employee has key cards, but system recognized them; if there is intensive contact between two departments, Google will place them closer to each other to increase efficiency.
  - **Counter-Example**: Chair of OM here at university.
    - Open space office rooms lead to distraction of all employees.
    - Open kitchen and restrooms lead to high traffic within the office and even increase distraction.
    - → Nobody can concentrate and only a few people still work there.

- **Layout Planning and Strategic Importance.**
  - Determination of long-term efficiency, has important long-term significance.
  - Establishes the company's priorities towards capacity, flexibility, costs and work life.
    - → Should be align with the business strategy.
  - Effective layout can lead to low costs, increased response time or differentiation.
  - Product characteristics determine the layout planning.

Customized products (e.g. super computer)	Requirements: High flexibility and on time delivery	Process focused layout (small batches because unique)
Standard products (e.g. TV)	Requirements: Cost minimization, efficiency maximization, fast delivery	Product focused layout (continuously production)

- **Basic Types of Layout Planning**
  - **Job Shop (process focused)**: Each product is unique.

- Jobs are divides into operations / tasks and departments responsible for each of them (painting, assembling).
- Frequency and sequence of tasks is very volatile, therefore flexibility is needed.
- Main concern is (constantly re-)arranging the departments (the higher the contact, the closer located).
- Objective is to simplify the workflow and increase efficiency.
- **Advantages**: Initial investment is relatively low, high flexibility.
  - Machinery break down won't delay production, other machines can overtake this task.
  - *Universal machinery*: can align to very different tasks, operating them requires high skills.
- **Disadvantages**: High organization effort, high unit costs, high-skilled employees needed.[2]

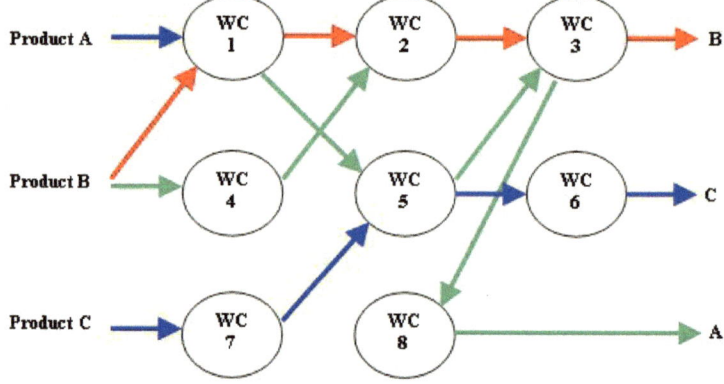

WC = Work Center

○ **Flow shop (product focused)**: Same type of product for many customers.
- Continuous production, same type of material and personnel flow.
- Departments are placed in order of production (= flow line).
→ Each production line is responsible for one product.
- Arrange several production lines in a facility.
- **Different Variations**:

2   Image Source: https://lh3.googleusercontent.com/-2JleJRXkhxE/UNpkvuF-6oI/AAAAAAAAAHA/EP0kuPGoBig/s519/job-shop.gif

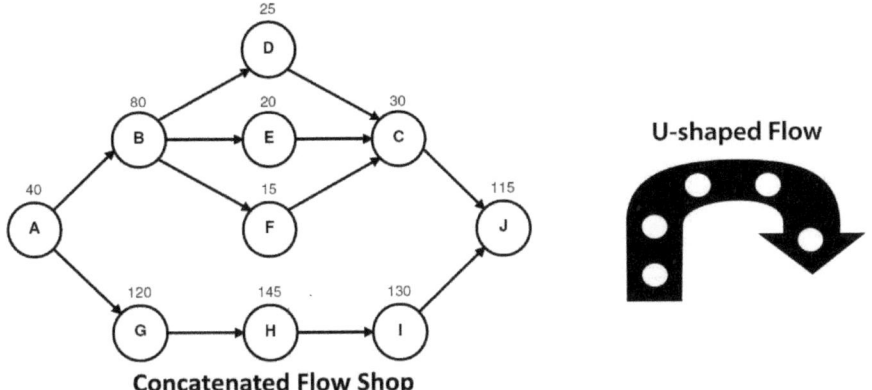

U-shaped Flow

Concatenated Flow Shop

- **U-shaped flow shop**: Due to physical constraints, production line is arranged as circle.
- → Optimize the space, minimize the coordination between workstation and departments.
- **Concatenated flow shop**: Different short flow lines are combined to one bigger one.
  - ○ Task J requires the parts from flow line 1 (B, E, C) and 2 (G, H, I) and task A produced one part that is needed for task B and G, but in the end only product J will be made.
- => Layout plan means occupation of the facility
- ▪ **Advantages**: Low unit costs, fast and efficient production.
- ▪ **Disadvantages**: Expensive, inflexible, changes in production line will cause costly delays.[3] [4]

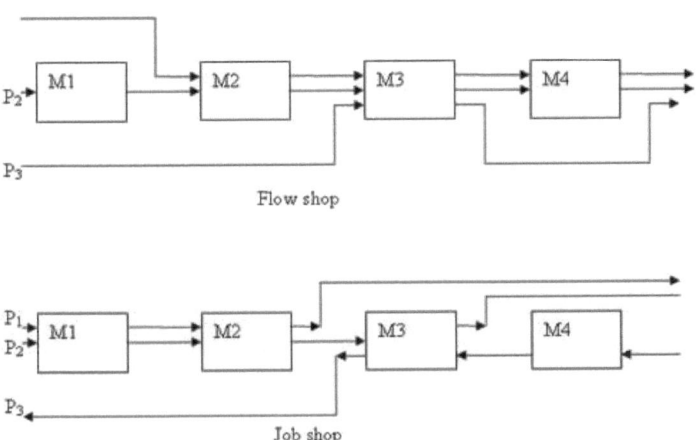

Flow shop

Job shop

- ○ **Cellular manufacturing (group technology layout)**: Intermediate form.
  - ▪ Building departments (called work cells) like in job shops, but inside follow a straight-line structure.
  - ▪ Some product parts are always standardized, will be produced within the departments, but

---

3   U-Shaped Image Source: http://image.thefabricator.com/a/making-lean-manufacturing-work-in-a-job-shop-2.jpg
4   Overview Image Source: http://www.rvholon.cimr.pub.ro/poze_control/job_flow_shop.jpg

connection of standardized parts to individual product occurs between the departments.
=> Very common due to the monopolistic competition in the markets.

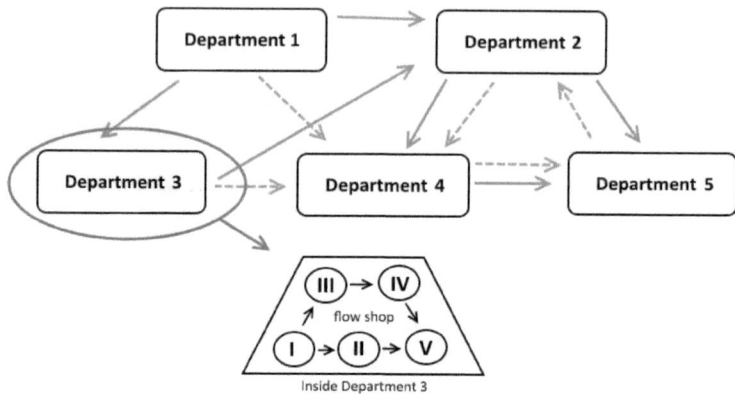

Inside Department 3

- **Example: Hospital.**
  - Job shop structure, all patients are unique, therefore flexible structure is needed.
  - Determine the different patterns and then find out a suitable layout.
  - Afterwards the layout can be criticized and re-arranged / optimized.

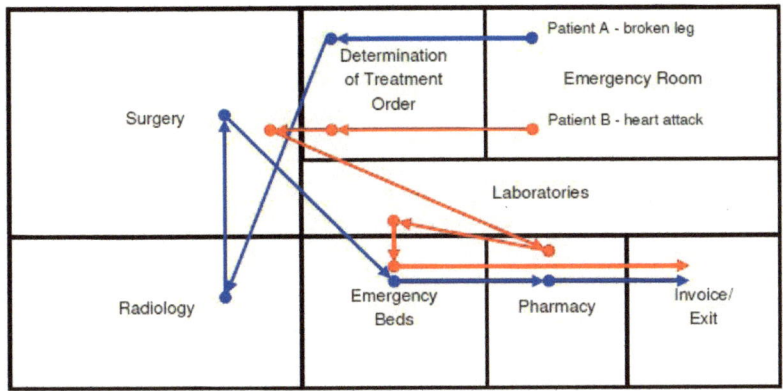

- **Systematic Layout Planing (SLP).**
  - **First step**: Determine a relationship chart (REL chart) between two departments for all departments.
  - **Second step**: All pairs receive a closeness rating. These six criteria are sufficient in the most cases.
  - **Third step**: Assign numerical values to each rating related to the preferences.
  - **Fourth step**: Calculate the total closeness rating of each department.

Rating	Definition	Numerical weight
A	Absolutely necessary	16
E	Especially important	8
I	Important	4
O	Ordinary closeness	2
U	Unimportant	0
X	Undesirable	-80

Dept.	1	2	3	4	5	6	A	E	I	O	U	X	TCR
1	0	E	O	I	X	A	1	1	1	1	0	1	-50
2	E	0	O	O	A	E	1	2	0	2	0	0	36
3	O	O	0	I	E	I	0	1	2	2	0	0	20
4	I	O	I	0	U	E	0	1	2	1	1	0	18
5	X	A	E	U	0	I	1	1	1	0	1	1	-52
6	A	E	I	E	I	0	1	2	2	0	0	0	40

  - TCR = Summed numerical values of the received ratings.
  - The higher the department is scored, the higher is its overall closeness to all other departments and the more important it should be treated in the layout planning.

- **Computerized Relationship Layout Planning CORELAP.**
  - Two steps of using the TCR to determine the optimal layout.
    - (1) Generating placement sequence.
    - (2) Determining the relative locations.
  - **Generating placement sequence.**
    - First department to be placed should have the highest TCR.
      - In case of several possible departments, chose the one with the most A grades.
    - Last department to be placed has an X relation with first department.
      - In case of several ones, chose the one with the lowest TCR as last one.
    - Second department has a A relation to the first one (in case of several ones: chose the one with

the highest TCR).
- Department to be placed before the last one has an X relation to the second one (chose the one with the lowest TCR last).
- **General Overview.**
  - Criteria for the first department: Highest TCR, most A grades.
  - Criteria second one: A relation to first one, highest TCR.
  - ...
  - Criteria for before-last departments: X-relation to second department and lowest TCR.
  - Criteria for last one: X-relation to first one and lowest TCR.
- ○ **Limitations of this method.**
  - If constraints are neglected, assign different numerical values to the grades and calculate layout again.
- ○ **Numerical Example.**

Dept.	1	2	3	4	5	6		A	E	I	O	U	X	TCR
1	0	E	O	I	X	A		1	1	1	1	0	1	-50
2	E	0	O	O	A	E		1	2	0	2	0	0	36
3	O	O	0	I	E	I		0	1	2	2	0	0	20
4	I	O	I	0	U	E		0	1	2	1	1	0	18
5	X	A	E	U	0	I		1	1	1	0	1	1	-52
6	A	E	I	E	I	0		1	2	2	0	0	0	40

- First: Department 6 (highest TCR).
- Second: 1 (A relation to 6).
- Last: 5 (X relation to 1).
- Third: 2 (E relation to 6 and 1).
- Forth: 4 (E relation to 6, I relation to 1).
- Fifth: 3 (remaining).
- => Placement sequence: {6, 1, 2, 4, 3, 5}.
- ○ **Determining the relative locations.**
  - Assumption: Each department has squared unit size.
  - Calculate weighted placement value (wpv) as sum of numerical values of neighboring departments.
  - Count possible department locations starting from the western edge counterclockwise.
- ○ **Numerical Example.**

subjective factors
fully adjacement: 1
partially adjacement: 0.5

8	7	6
1	6	5
2	3	4

fully adjacement: 1, 3, 5, 7
partially adjacement: 2, 4, 6, 8
Freely chose 1, 3, 5 or 7 because
equal wpv, chose western edge 1

10	9	8	7
1	1	6	6
2	3	4	5

first view reveals 3, 4, 8, 9 as best locations
wpv is the same, chose the one with
lowest number assigned, 3

12	11	10	9
1	1	6	8
2	2	6	7
3	4	5	

to be excluded 3, 5, 7, 9, 12
to be calculated 1, 2, 4, 6, 8, 10, 11
wpv of 6 = 0.5 * 4 + 1 * 2 + 1 * 8 = 12

- **Differences Process and Product Layout.**
  - ○ Process layout: arrange departments (distance between related departments should be minimized).
  - ○ Product layout: balance the flow (tasks assigned to each department should be balanced).

- **Product Layout Planning.**
  - ○ Assumptions.
    - ▪ Volume lead to high capacity utilization.
    - ▪ Demand is stable and high.
    - ▪ Product is standardized and in growth phase or maturity.
      => Justify the high investment of a flow shop
    - ▪ Supply of input is on time and quality of goods always the same.
      → Ensure continuous flow of goods.
    - ▪ Common assumption: Equal processing time for all workstations.
  - ○ **Assembly Line Balancing.**
    - ▪ Product-focused layout designs, inflexible, high investment, most efficient.
    - ▪ Process of dividing work into least amount of workstations to ensure minimization of downtime.
      - • Workstation is physical are where worker or machine performs one specific set of tasks.
        - ○ Same idea as departments, but in here several tasks can be performed.
      - • Work centers group similar workstations together.
        => Overall objective is to minimize idle time and keep the amount of workstations as low as possible to ensure this.
  - ○ **Workstations.**
    - ▪ Several tasks are needed to perform one product, but some tasks can and should be grouped

into one single work station.

→ Total number of workstations should be lower than total number of tasks.

- After one workstation has finished it work, it can hand its parts to other workstations for the next procedure → Ensure that the flow of material has as few pauses as possible.

=> Grouping tasks into workstations means taking correlations into account.

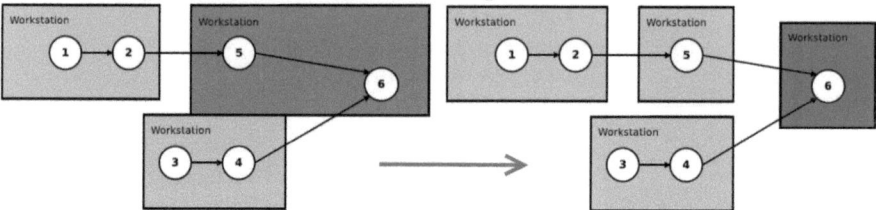

- **Overview on Assembly Line Balancing.**
  - (1) Divide standard product into single tasks.
  - (2) Determine the order or sequence of performance.
  - (3) Draw precedence diagram → Flowchart.
  - (4) Estimate task times (given).
  - (5) Calculate cycle times.
  - (6) Calculate the minimum number of workstations.
  - (7) Use heuristic to balance assembly line (good solution, not best).
  - **Parameter Constraints.**
    - Cycle time and quantity are key numbers and must fit into a predetermined interval.
    - **Cycle time constraints.**
      - Lower bound: Maximum processing time.
        - No task can be further divided, no reduction of time possible anymore.
      - Upper bound: Production rate to guarantee productivity.
    - **Quantity constraints.**
      - Lower bound = upper bound of cycle time = $\sum\limits_{i=1}^{l} \dfrac{d_i}{c_{max}} = M$ = number of workstations.
      - Upper bound: Total number of operations.
  - Production rate: $x = \dfrac{1}{c} = \dfrac{1}{cycle\ time}$.
  - Completion time: $C = M * c$.
  - Idle time: $I = C - \sum\limits_{i=1}^{l} d_i$.
  - Efficiency: $E = \dfrac{\sum\limits_{i=1}^{l} d_1}{M * c}$ [%].
  - **Numerical Example.**
    - Production time: 8 hours / day.
    - Required quantity: 100 units a day.
    - $C_{Max} = \dfrac{8\ hours\,/\,day * 60\ minutes}{100\ units\,/\,day} = 4.8\ minutes\ per\ unit$.

- **Process of Positional Weight Approach.**
  - (1) Determine priorities of the operations.
  - (2) Open a new workstation.

20

- (3) Select the most important task (start with the most important one, first in a row).
- (4) Assign to a workstation if precedence and cycle time constraints are fitting.
- (5) Otherwise open a new workstation for this task.
- **Numerical Example.**

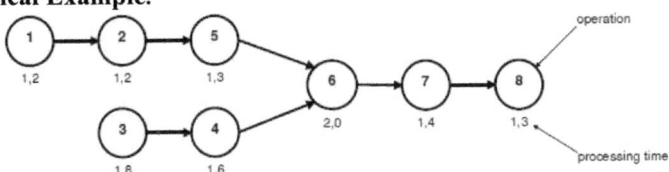

- 8 tasks, x = 140 units per day, production time = 420 minutes per day.
- Task is to determine each workstation cycle time and to minimize the number of workstations.
- **(1) Cycle time constraints.**
  - Lower bound: Maximum task time, here 2.0 because task 6 needs this time for sure.
  - Upper bound: $\dfrac{production\ time}{required\ quantity} = \dfrac{420}{140} = 3\ minutes\ per\ unit$.
  - => Cycle time interval = {2, 3}.
- **(2) Heuristic: "Most following tasks".**
  - Only one possible heuristic, others are also possible.
  - Opposite is exact approach (dynamic programming), comparing all possible combinations and evaluate them by their efficiency (see below).
  - Set up a table to illustrate by how many tasks each task is followed.

Task	1	2	3	4	5	6	7	8
# following	5	4	4*	3	3	2	1	-
Priority	1	2	2	3	3	4	5	6

  - Task 3 is essential for task 4 (direct relation) and 6, 7, and 8 (indirect relation).
- **(3) Assign each task into workstations in relation to it's priority and processing time.**

Station	Task	Task Time	Remaining Time	Sum of task times	Candidate List	Explanations
1					{1, 3}*	* Both have no previous tasks
	1'	1.2	1.8#	1.2	{2, 3}	' higher priority than 3
	2	1.2	0.6	2.4	{5, 3}	# C$_{max}$ – processing time
2	3*	1.8	1.2	1.2	{5, 4}	* not enough remaining time in S1
3	4	1.6	1.4	1.6	{5}	* new C$_{max}$, more efficient than old
	5	1.3	0.1	2.9*	{6}	one
4	6	2.0	1.0	2.0	{7}	
5	7	1.4	1.6	1.4	{8}	
	8	1.3	0.3	2.7	{/}	

- **(4) Determine the optimal layout.**

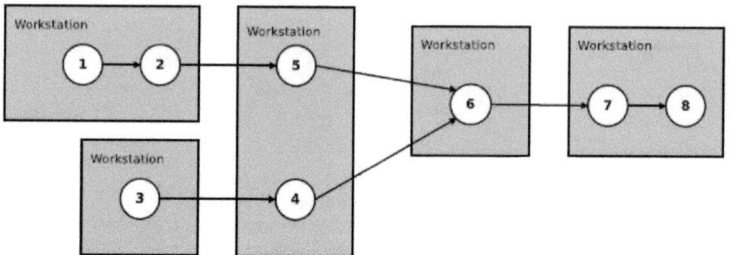

- **(5) Calculate related key numbers for this layout.**
  - Maximum task time is 2.9 minutes.
  - **Production rate:** $\frac{420}{2.9} = 144.83 > 140$.
  - **Idle time:** $2.9 - 2.4 + 2.9 - 1.2 + 2.9 - 2.9 + 2.9 - 2.0 + 2.9 - 2.7 = 2.7$.
  - **Elapsed time:** $5 * 2.9 = 14.5$ minutes for each product.
  - **Efficiency:** $E = \dfrac{elapsed\ time - idle\ time}{elapsed\ time} = \dfrac{14.5 - 2.7}{14.5} = 81.38\% > 80\%$ (acceptable).
  - $\rightarrow$ Key number to compare different layouts with each other.

- **Basic Model of Production Planning.**
  - ○ Has to be combined with inventory management; core of operations management.
  - ○ Assumptions:
    - Consideration of one single period (one production cycle).
    - Other products are existing, competing for resources.
    - Maximization of profits while prices and variable unit costs remain constant.
    - Existence of a bottleneck, products are competing, no production of infinity units.
      $\Rightarrow$ Question is how to assign resources to the different production lines to maximize profits.
  - ○ **Mathematical Formalization.**
    - **Maximize the profit:** $\displaystyle\sum_{j=1}^{J} g_j * x_j$ g = profit of unit j; x = respective quantity.
    - **Capacity constraint:** $\displaystyle\sum_{j=1}^{J} a_{ij} * x_j \leq T_i$ resource i needed for total quantity of product j must

    be smaller of equal the total capacity of resource i.
    - **Non-negativity**: Production quantity can't be negative.
      $\Rightarrow$ Linear Model, solve by Simplex.
  - ○ **Numerical Example.**

Machine	Processing time prod 1	Processing time prod 2	Max. Capacity
1	6	2	480
2	10	10	1000
3	1	4	280

  - And with additional information of prices for products € 10 and € 20, we have a set of equations.
  - Overall **objective function**: *Maximize g $(x, y) = 10x + 20y$* .

22

- **Constraints**: $6x + 2y \leq 480$, $10x + 10y \leq 1000$, $x + 4y \leq 280$ and $x, y \geq 0$.
- **Graphical Solution.**
  - Make the inequalities to equal signs and set one variable to 0 to determine the intersection with the respective axis and then repeat with the other variable.
  - Like this: $6x + 2y = 480 \rightarrow 6x + 2*0 = 480 \rightarrow x = 80$, $6*0 + 2y = 480 \rightarrow y = 240$.
  - Total graph will look like this.

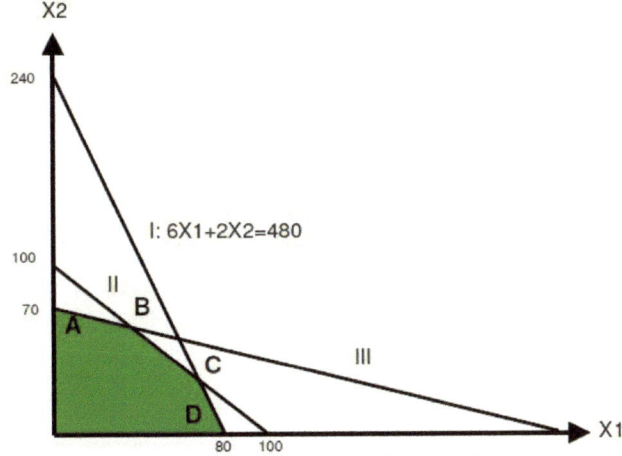

- Every point within the green shaded area is a possible / feasible point.
- We know that only corner solutions are profit maximizing, so calculate respective profits for points A, B, C, and D.
  => Point B = (40, 60) reveals the highest profit g (40, 60) = 1600.
- **Solve by Simplex.**
  - Overall **objective function**: *Maximize g* $(x, y) = 10x + 20y$.
  - **Constraints**: $6x + 2y \leq 480$, $10x + 10y \leq 1000$, $x + 4y \leq 280$ and $x, y \geq 0$.
    - Turn the constraints into equations by introduction of slack variables.
      - $6x + 2y + z_1 = 480$, $10x + 10y + z_2 = 1000$, $x + 4y + z_3 = 280$.
  - Arrange the Simplex Tableau.
    - On the left side, insert the slack variables and the negative variables of the objective function.
    - On the right side (above) insert the important variables followed by the slack variables.

BV	x	y	Z_1	Z_2	Z_3	T
Z_1	6	2	1	0	0	480
Z_2	10	10	0	1	0	1000
Z_3	1	4	0	0	1	280
OF	-10	-20	0	0	0	0

- Take the column with the highest negative number of the objective function.
- Take the number within this column with the lowest ratio of T/number.
- (1) Set all numbers over and under the 4 to 0.
- (2) Divide all numbers right and left the 4 by 4.
- (3) Change the numbers in the green colored fields.
- (4) Repeat this procedure until no variable in the

$$-10 - \frac{(-20) * 1}{4} = -5$$

23

objective function is negative anymore.

BV	x	y	Z_1	Z_2	Z_3	T
Z_1	0	0	1	-0.733	-4/3	120
x	1	0	0	0.133	-1/3	40
y	0	1	0	-0.033	1/3	60
OF	0	0	0	2/3	10/3	1600

=> Optimal quantities are x = 40 and y = 60 , profit is 1600.

- **Multi-period Production Program Planning.**
  - ○ Planning horizon is extended, demand has to be forecasted for each period.
  - ○ Either produce products to satisfy demand or take them from the inventory.
    - ▪ Trade-off between the strategies of **Synchronization** and **Emancipation**.
      - → The intermediate form is most commonly used.
  - ○ Given the number of periods and the respective demand forecasts, we can calculate average demand each day (synchronization) and average production each period (emancipation).

Month	Demand	Cum. Demand	Prod. Days	Average demand/day	Average production	Cum. production
Jan	900	900	22	41	1100	1100
Feb	1000	1900	18	56	900	2000
Mar	1500	3400	21	71	1050	3050
Apr	1200	4600	21	57	1050	4100
May	800	5400	22	36	1100	5200
Jun	800	6200	20	40	1000	6200
			124			
Average production: 50/day						

- ○ Average demand / day = $\dfrac{demand}{production\ days} = \dfrac{900}{22} = 41$.
- ○ Average production = $average\ production * production\ days = 50 * 22 = 1100$.
- ○ This kind of production planning is often used by small or medium-size companies.
  - ▪ Either follow synchronization (average demand / day) or emancipation (average production).
- ○ In case of synchronization, sometimes goods have to be stored or demand is not satisfied.
  - → Related to (high) costs.

Synchronisation:

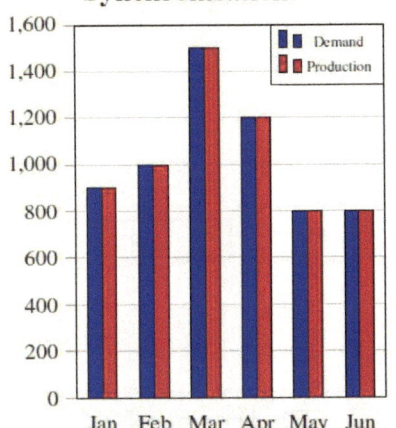

Emancipation:

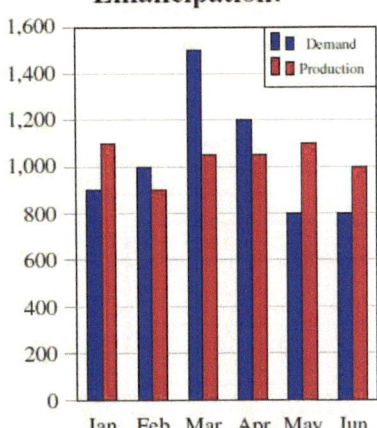

- ○ Important Inventory Formula: $y_{jk} = y_{jk-1} + x_{jk} - r_{jk}$.
  - ■ Inventory at the end of this period is equal to inventory at the end of the last period + production in this period – sales in this period.
    - → Linear equation, no inequality, therefore very hard for software to solve.
    - => Enter the field of Inventory Management, considering such concerns.

- **Inventory Management.**

  - ○ Inventory function: $y_t = y_0 + \sum_{k=0}^{t} (x_k - r_k)$.

  y_k = inventory at the end of period k
  x_k = production quantity of period k
  r_k = demand of period k

  - ○ Definition: Inventory is a system whose state is determined by replenishments (order quantity) and demand.
  - ○ **Kinds of Inventory.**
    - ■ **Working Stock**: Inventory held in advance of demand for economic reasons (quantity discount).
    - ■ **Safety Stock**: Inventory held in advance of demand to protect for uncertainties.
    - ■ **Anticipation Stock**: Inventory held in advance of demand to face upcoming demand shifts (seasonal fluctuations, machine maintenance, events occurring for sure).
    - ■ **Pipeline Stock**: Inventory which is constantly moving and not available (on trucks or between workstations).
    - ■ **Decoupling Stock**: Inventory held to be secure of delays of all kinds.

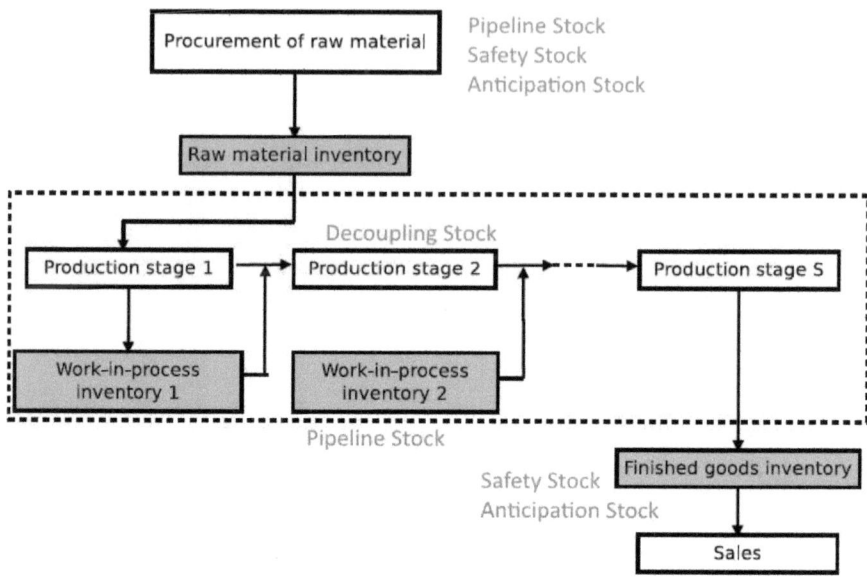

- **Costs of Inventory.**
  - *Fixed costs*: rent for facilities, heating costs → Not crucial for optimal inventory level.
  - *Fixed ordering costs*: administration costs, shipping charges.
    - → Induces to order large quantities.
  - *Variable costs*: depending on quantity and duration of storage.
    - → Induces to have small quantities.
    - => Trade-off, Inventory management has to balance both factors.
  - *Shortage costs.*
    - **Lost Sales**: In case of not meeting actual demand, hard to quantity, lost customers maybe also lost in the future.
    - **Back orders**: If unsatisfied demand is delivered with delay (costs of rebates, extra bookkeeping, time value).

- **The ABC-Analysis.**
  - Determine which kind of input is essentially for the production (A-goods) or can be handled by standardized processes (B- & C-goods).
  - How to perform an ABC-analysis.
  - Given information:
    - Required units per period and unit costs.

Item	Annual usage	Unit costs
1	40,000	0.07
2	195,000	0.11
3	4,000	0.1
4	100,000	0.05
5	2,000	0.14

6	240,000	0.07
7	16,000	0.08
8	80,000	0.06
9	10,000	0.07
10	5,000	0.09

○ (1) Calculate the total periodic costs and rank them, starting with the highest value.

Item	1	2	3	4	5	6	7	8	9	10
Annual cost	2,800	21,450	400	5,000	280	16,800	1,280	4,800	700	450
Rank	5	1	9	3	10	2	6	4	7	8

○ (2) Calculate the percentage value of periodic costs of one product to total periodic costs.

Rank	1	2	3	4	5	6	7	8	9	10
Annual cost	21,450	16,800	5,000	4,800	2,800	1,280	700	450	400	280
%	39.8	31.1	9.3	8.8	5.2	2.4	1.3	0.8	0.8	0.5
Cum. %	39.8	70.9	80.2	89.0	94.2	96.6	97.9	98.7	99.5	100

○ (3) Set up a Lorenz-Curve to determine the goods.
- Determining 70 – 80% of the whole costs are A-goods.
- Determining less than 10% are C-goods.
  → Everything in between are B-goods.

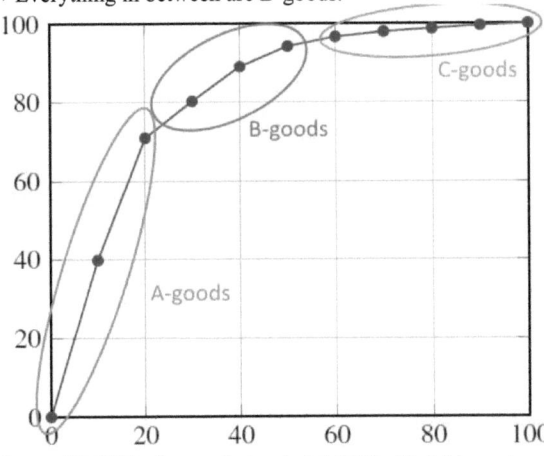

○ A-Items: 75-80% of costs, but only 15-20% of total inventory parts.
- Constant review on inventory level, most personalized control / treatment, highest attention.
○ B-Items: 10-20% of costs, but only 20-25% of total inventory parts.
- Moderate, but sill significant effort / attention needed.

- ○ C-Items: Only 5-10% of costs, but 60-65% of inventory parts.
  - ▪ Group all parts together and use same policy, calculate optimal order quantity for all of them, storage costs are neglectable, minimize managerial effort.

- **XYZ-Analysis.**
  - ○ X-Items: Constant, predictable demand.
  - ○ Y-Items: Fluctuations and trend-line pattern, medium predictability.
  - ○ Z-Items: Completely irregular usage (luxury articles or decoupling stock).

- **Types of Procurement.**
  - ○ **A & X-Items: Just-in-Time-Procurement**: Strategy of Synchronization, cost minimization, no inventory costs, requires delivery in time and highly efficient processes; demand is predictable therefore planning is easy.
  - ○ **B, C & Y-Items: Stock Procurement**: Use EOQ to determine optimal order quantity, working stock, prepare for uncertainties.

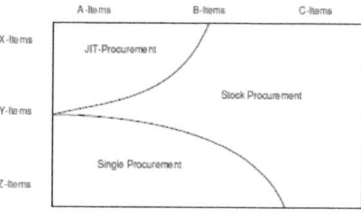

  - ○ **A, B & Z-Items: Single Procurement**: Only after concrete order, the parts are bought, shortage time occurs, customers must be willing to wait for product, safety stock not applicable because A-items will cause too high costs in storehouses.

- **Classic Model of Inventory Management.**
  - ○ EOQ Model (supply management): order the same quantity each period, replenishment will arrive immediately.
    - ▪ Basic assumptions: constant demand, no transportation time & risks.

    - ▪ $$Q_{optimal} = \sqrt{\frac{2 * c_B * x_v}{c_L}}$$

      With c_B = fixed order costs,
      x_v = demand rate in units per time
      c_L = inventory carrying costs per unit and time (inventory storage costs)

  - ○ EPQ Model (production planning): produce quantity required for each period, immediately the quantity from one workstation is transferred to the sequential workstation.
    - ▪ Same basic assumption like in EOQ.
    - ▪ In reality production time differs among workstations and will cause idle time.
      - → Time supply of raw material so that idle time is minimized.

- **Inventory Management – Service Level.**
  - ○ Extension of the basic model.
  - ○ Uncertainties, changes in demand and lead time due to bottlenecks are considered.
    - → Stock-outs / Shortages will occur.
  - ○ Introduce safety stock, but how many units?
    - ▪ Problem is evaluation of shortage costs (lost customers and back order costs).
  - ○ Normally demand is relatively stable, but sometimes the demand exceeds the overall capacities and in such cases the safety stock is used.
    - ▪ Is held at a constant level to minimize shortage costs; safety stock is a fixed asset.
  - ○ **Service Level Model.**

- Take all relevant data from past observations and find an adequate density function.
- Describe the average 8mean) and standard deviation to calculate the optimal formula.
- Plot the graph.
- If ordering time s is equal to expected lead time demand, the shortage probability will be 50%.
- If s is placed unequal to expected lead time demand, the probability will decrease.
  → Normally target a certain probability (quantile like the value of risk).

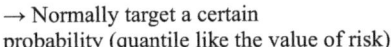
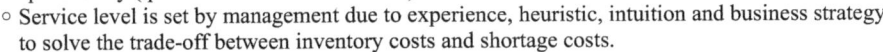

- ○ Service level is set by management due to experience, heuristic, intuition and business strategy to solve the trade-off between inventory costs and shortage costs.
  - Normally around 70% but for more valuable clients can be up to 95%.
  - High service level indicates high probability of completely satisfaction of demand, but also higher inventory costs.
    => Empirical study reveals that increasing service level above 90% will dramatically increase the inventory costs.

- **Optimal Safety Stock in discrete case.**
  - ○ Given information: demand during lead time and frequency of occurrence, service level (here: 75%).

Demand	2	3	4	5	6	7	8	9
Amount	2	6	11	8	4	2	1	1

  - ○ **(1) Determine the optimal order point.**
    - Calculate the probability and cumulative probabilities of occurrence.

Actual DDLT	Frequency	Probability	Cum. Probability
2	2	2/35	$2/35 \approx 0.0571$
3	6	6/35	$8/35 \approx 0.2286$
4	11	11/35	$19/35 \approx 0.5429$
5	8	8/35	$27/35 \approx 0.7714$
6	4	4/35	$31/35 \approx 0.8857$
7	2	2/35	$33/35 \approx 0.9439$
8	1	1/35	$34/35 \approx 0.9714$
9	1	1/35	$35/35 = 1$
	Σ 35		

  - Colored area means: For more than 77% of all times, the DDLT has been 5 units or less.
    → To achieve the service level of 75%, choose therefore 5 units safety stock.
  - Order point is s = 5.
  - ○ **(2) Determine the expected DDLT.**
    - Sum of actual DDLT times probability of occurrence.

- $$EDDLT = 2 * \frac{2}{35} + 3 * \frac{6}{35} + 4 * \frac{11}{35} + 5 * \frac{8}{35} + 6 * \frac{4}{35} + 7 * \frac{2}{35} + 8 * \frac{1}{35} + 9 * \frac{1}{35} = 4.6 \quad .$$
  - ○ **(3) Effective Level of Safety Stock.**
    - $Safety\ Stock = s - EDDLT = 5 - 4.6 = 0.4$.
    - Because result is strongly mathematical and hard to transmit into reality, calculate a percentage value regarding the safety stock $\frac{0.4}{5} = 0.08 = 8\%$.

- **Optimal Safety Stock in continuous case.**
  - ○ Given information: mean demand (here: 693.7), standard deviation of demand (here: 139.27), service level (here: 95%).
    - We are transforming our normal distribution into a standard normal distribution and search for the quartil; therefore search in the table for the corresponding value for 0.95.
    - Its between 1.64 and 1.65; in such a case, always choose the lower value.
    - Now insert this number into the "undo-standardization" formula $s = mean + z * sigma$ and find the optimal order point.
    - $s = 693.7 + 1.64 * 139.27 = 922.10$, the optimal safety stock amount is simply z * sigma, here 228.4.

Guideline: How to solve different exercises?

- **(I) Decision Trees.**
  - ○ Needed Information:
    - Deposit rate: h = 6%
    - Debt interest rate: s = 12%
    - Payoffs faced when undertaking no action = {65, -10, 90}.
    - Action plan and related costs.

Action	Costs	
	t = 0	t = 1
Small Expansion	50	
Big Expansion	90	
Additional small expansion		25
Reduction of big expansion		-20
No action		0

- Scenario analysis for demand and related probabilities of occurrence.

Demand	Capacity		Demand in 1st period	Demand in 2nd period
	low	high	low $P(L) = 60\%$	low $P(L|L) = 50\ \%$
low	50	50		high $P(H|L) = 50\%$
high	50	100	high $P(H) = 40\%$	low $P(L|H) = 20\%$
				high $P(H|H) = 80\%$

- ○ (1) Set up the static scenario analysis to determine possible alternatives.
  - In period 0 you can either chose to do a small expansion or a big one.
  - Related to your decision in period 0, you can chose another action or no further one in period 1.

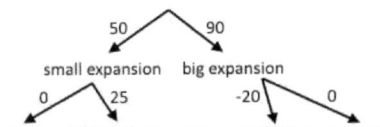

  - Don't forget to assign numbers to each alternative (each path).
- ○ (2) Set up the scenario analysis for the possible demand scenarios.
  - Demand can be high or low in both periods, with certain probabilities.
- ○ (3) Combine both tree diagrams into one big one.

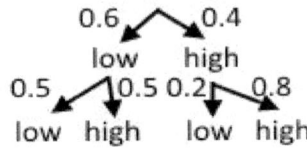

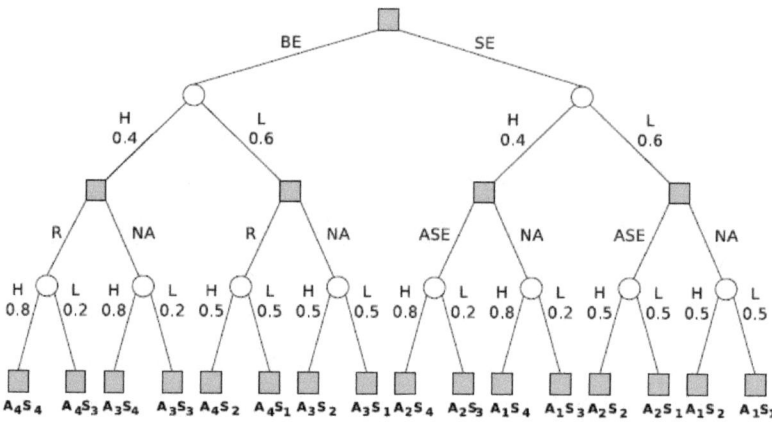

- (4) Calculate the value of each path.
  - A_4S_4: Do a big investment (costs 90), face high demand (capacity 100), reduce expansion (gain 20), face high demand again (capacity 50).
    - Getting 65 in period 0 and spend 90 means lending 25 for 12% (payback next period 28).
    - Facing high demand in next period and getting 100, regular profit is -10, payback of previous period is 28, reduction will provide additional 20.
      - Cash Flow of period 1: $100 - 10 - 28 + 20 = 82$ deposited for 6%
        $\rightarrow$ Starting with 86.92 in next period.
    - Facing high demand, but having reduced capacity means getting 50, regular profit is 90.
      - Cash Flow of period 2: $86.92 + 50 + 90 = 226.92$
  - A_2S_4: Do a small investment (costs 50), face high demand (capacity 50), do an additional investment (cost 25), face high demand again (capacity 100).
    - Getting 65 in period 0, spending 50 for investments means 15 can be deposited.
      $\rightarrow$ Starting with $15 * 1.06 = 15.9$ next period.
    - Getting -10 in period 1, spending 25 for additional investment and facing demand of 50.
      - Cash Flow in period 1: $15.9 - 10 - 25 + 50 = 30.9$ (starting with 32.75 next period).
    - Getting 90 in period 2 and facing demand of 100.
      - Cash Flow of period 2: $32.75 + 90 + 100 = 222.75$
- (5) Calculate the weighted average for each alternative over all scenarios and find the highest expected capital value.
  $\rightarrow$ This alternative will yield the highest capital value.
  - **ECV for alternative 2**: 172.754 * 0.3 (Prob for Low Low) + 222.754 * 0.3 (Prob for Low High) + 172.754 * 0.08 (Prob for High Low) + 222.754 * 0.32 (Prob for High High) = 203.754.
  - It can also be possible to set up a decision tree for costs, in this case you have to chose the lowest average value.

	S_1	S_2	S_3	S_4	ECV
A_1	199.25	199.25	199.25	199.25	199.25
A_2	172.754	222.754	172.754	222.754	203.754
A_3	152.72	202.72	205.72	255.72	204.92*
A_4	173.92	173.92	226.92	226.92	195.12

- **(II) Experience Curves.**
  - Needed Information:
    - Doublings of production quantities.
    - Costs of respective last units.
    - Formula at the side.

$$b = \frac{n \cdot \sum_{i=1}^{n} (x_i \cdot y_i) - \sum_{i=1}^{n} x_i \cdot \sum_{i=1}^{n} y_i}{n \cdot \sum_{i=1}^{n} x_i^2 - \left(\sum_{i=1}^{n} x_i\right)^2} \qquad a = \frac{\sum_{i=1}^{n} y_i \cdot \sum_{i=1}^{n} x_i^2 - \sum_{i=1}^{n} (y_i \cdot x_i) \cdot \sum_{i=1}^{n} x_i}{n \cdot \sum_{i=1}^{n} x_i^2 - \left(\sum_{i=1}^{n} x_i\right)^2}$$

$$k_X = k_1 X^{-b} \longrightarrow \ln(k_{(X)}) = \ln(k_1) - b\ln(X) \longrightarrow k_{(X)}^* = k_1^* - bX^*$$

i	x	$k(x)$	$\ln x$	$\ln k(x)$	$[\ln x]^2$	$\ln x \cdot \ln k(x)$
1	1	78	0	4.3567		
2	2	64	0.6931	4.1589		
3	4	47	1.3863	3.8501		
4	8	42	2.0794	3.7377		
5	16	41	2.7725	3.7136		
6	32	31	3.4567	3.4340		
7	64	26	4.1589	3.2581		
8	128	22	4.8520	3.1410		
9	256	20	5.5452	2.9957	30.7490	16.6119
10	512	17	6.2383	2.8332		
Sum			31.1916	35.4291	136.9291	101.0242

=> With this data, simply insert into the formulae above and estimate the parameters.
- Don't forget to undo the linearization mentioned in the long formula.
  - Estimator for $\hat{a}$ needs to be taken e^x because it is only the ln of real $\hat{a}$.
  - (1) Calculate $\hat{b}$ with the formula and data from above.

$$\hat{b} = \frac{10*101.0242 - 31.1916*35.4291}{10*16.9291 - (31.1916)^2} = 0.2392 \quad.$$

  - (2) Calculate $\hat{k}_1$.

$$\hat{k}_1^{\hat{}} = \frac{35.4291*16.9291 - 101.0242*31.1916}{10*16.9291 - (31.1916)^2} = 4.28292 \quad.$$

  - (3) Undo the linearization for $\hat{k}_1$.

$$k_1 = e^{\hat{k}_1} = e^{4.28292} = 72.9147 \quad.$$

  - (4) Set up the linear regression equation → Experience curve.

$$k_{(X)} = 72.9147 * X^{-0.2392} \quad.$$

- **(III) Systematic Layout Planing (SLP) & Computerized Relationship Layout Planning CORELAP.**
  - Given information:
    - Relationship chart (relation between all departments) (in the exercise already inserted into a table (see step 2)).
    - Subjective numerical values for closeness grades.
    - Subjective factors for weighted placement value (wpv) calculation.

Rating	Definition	Numerical weight
A	Absolutely necessary	16
E	Especially important	8
I	Important	4
O	Ordinary closeness	2
U	Unimportant	0
X	Undesirable	-80

  - (1) Determine the grades for each pair of departments.
  - (2) List the total amount of each grade received by one department and sum the numerical values for each grade.

Dept.	1	2	3	4	5	6		A	E	I	O	U	X	TCR
1	0	E	O	I	X	A		1	1	1	1	0	1	-50
2	E	0	O	O	A	E		1	2	0	2	0	0	36
3	O	O	0	I	E	I		0	1	2	2	0	0	20
4	I	O	I	0	U	E		0	1	2	1	1	0	18
5	X	A	E	U	0	I		1	1	1	0	1	1	-52
6	A	E	I	E	I	0		1	2	2	0	0	0	40

- (3) Generate the placing sequence.
  - Determine which department to be placed first, which second, … and which last.
  - Criteria for determining the placing sequence.
    - Criteria for the first department: Highest TCR, most A grades.
    - Criteria second one: A relation to first one, highest TCR.
    - …
    - Criteria for before-last departments: X-relation to second department and lowest TCR.
    - Criteria for last one: X-relation to first one and lowest TCR.
  - Department 6 has highest TCR, therefore will be placed first.
  - Department 1 has A relationship with 6, therefore placed second.
  - Department 5 has X relationship with 1, therefore placed last.
  - Department 2 has E relation to 1 and 6, placed third.
  - Department 4 has E relation to 1, E relation to 6, O relation to 2, place fourth.
  - Department 3 place fifth because its remaining.
  - => Placement sequence: {6, 1, 2, 4, 3, 5}.
- (4) Determine the relative location with the weighted placement value.
  - *Suppose the subjective factor for fully adjacement: 1, for partially adjacement 0.5.*
  - (I) Place the first department and assign numbers counterclockwise for the possible locations around it, starting from the Western side.

8	7	6
1	6	5
2	3	4

  - Fully adjacent are locations 1, 3, 5, 7; others are only partially adjacent.
    → WPV for those locations must be equally high.
  - WPV (location 1) = relation between placed department and department to be placed next x subjective factor for fully adjacement = 16 * 1 = 16.
    → In case of several possibilities due to same wpv, assign new department to location with the smallest number.
  - (II) After placing the second department, again, assign numbers to the locations surrounding both placed departments the same way as mentioned before.

10	9	8	7
1	1	6	6
2	3	4	5

  - Exclude by first-view: 2, 5, 7, 10 because only partially adjacent to one department.
  - Calculate wpv for locations 1, 3, 4, 6, 8, and 9.
    → Due to the same grades between department 2 and 1 and 2 and 6, locations 3, 4, 8, 9 have the same wpv (wpv (3) = 8 * 1 + 8 * 0.5 = 12).
  - (III) Repeat until all departments are placed.

- **(IV) Assembly Line Balancing & Positional Weight Approach.**
  - Given information:
    - Figure of relation between each task.
    - Processing time of each task.
    - Required production quantity each period (here: 140 units / day).
    - Production time each period (here: 420 minutes / day).
    - Given heuristic (here: most following tasks).

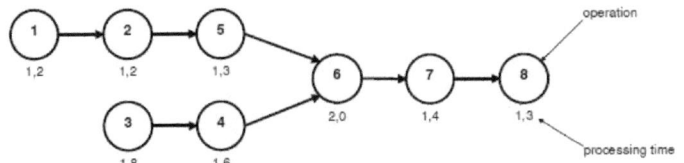

- ○ **(1) Calculate the cycle time constraints.**
  - ▪ C_{Min} = maximum processing time of one task, here 2.0 minutes (task 6).
  - ▪ $C_{Max} = \dfrac{production\ time}{required\ quantity} = \dfrac{420}{140} = 3\ minutes\ per\ unit$.
  - => Cycle time interval = {2.0 ; 3.0}.
- ○ **(2) Assign priorities to each task due to the heuristic.**
  - ▪ Given the heuristic "most following tasks", we have to determine how many tasks are following each single task and assign the highest priority to the one with the most following tasks.

Task	1	2	3	4	5	6	7	8
# following	5	4	4*	3	3	2	1	-
Priority	1	2	2	3	3	4	5	6

  - ○ Task 3 is essential for task 4 (direct relation) and 6, 7, and 8 (indirect relation).
- ○ **(3) Assign each task into workstations.**
  - ▪ Determine the possible candidates, here: start with the tasks which don't need previous production steps = {1, 3}.
  - ▪ Assign the task with the higher priority to the first workstation (WS) and calculate the remaining time in this workstation.
  - • C_{Max} – processing time of this task = 3.0 – 1.2 = 1.8.
  - ▪ Again determine the next possible candidates and check whether they fit into this workstation or if you have to open another one.
  - ▪ Repeat this procedure until you've assigned each task into workstations.

Station	Task	Task Time	Remaining Time	Sum of task times	Candidate List
1					{1, 3}*
	1'	1.2	1.8#	1.2	{2, 3}
	2	1.2	0.6	2.4	{5, 3}
2	3*	1.8	1.2	1.2	{5, 4}
3	4	1.6	1.4	1.6	{5}
	5	1.3	0.1	2.9*	{6}
4	6	2.0	1.0	2.0	{7}
5	7	1.4	1.6	1.4	{8}
	8	1.3	0.3	2.7	{/}

- • **(4) Evaluate the usefulness of this layout by calculating the key numbers.**
  - ○ Maximum task time is 2.9 minutes.
  - ○ **Production rate:** $\dfrac{420}{2.9} = 144.83 > 140$.
  - ○ **Idle time:** $2.9 - 2.4 + 2.9 - 1.2 + 2.9 - 2.9 + 2.9 - 2.0 + 2.9 - 2.7 = 2.7$.
  - ○ **Elapsed time:** $5 * 2.9 = 14.5$ minutes for each product.

- ○ **Efficiency:** $E = \dfrac{elapsed\ time - idle\ time}{elapsed\ time} = \dfrac{14.5 - 2.7}{14.5} = 81.38\% > 80\%$ (acceptable).
  → Key number to compare different layouts with each other.

- **(V) Basic Model of Production Planning – Simplex Solution.**
  - ○ Given information:
    - Prices of both outcomes (€ 10 and € 20).
    - Possible machines with different constraints (here: time constraints) being able to produce both outcomes, but face limitations (here: capacity limitations).

Machine	Processing time prod 1	Processing time prod 2	Max. Capacity
1	6	2	480
2	10	10	1000
3	1	4	280

- ○ **(1) Set up respective formulae out of this table.**
  - Overall **objective function**: *Maximize* $g(x, y) = 10x + 20y$.
  - **Constraints**: $6x + 2y \le 480$, $10x + 10y \le 1000$, $x + 4y \le 280$ and $x, y \ge 0$.
- ○ **(2) Turn all inequations into equations by inserting slack variables.**
  - $6x + 2y + z_1 = 480$, $10x + 10y + z_2 = 1000$, $x + 4y + z_3 = 280$.
- ○ **(3) Set up the Simplex Tableau.**
  - Insert on the left side all slack variables, above the important variables and then the slack variables and then type in all constraints.
  - Variables of objective formula turned negative.

BV	x	y	Z_1	Z_2	Z_3	T
Z_1	6	2	1	0	0	480
Z_2	10	10	0	1	0	1000
Z_3	1	4	0	0	1	280
OF	-10	-20	0	0	0	0

- ○ **(4) Solve the Simplex Tableau.**
  - In the line for the objective function shouldn't appear any negative number anymore.
  - Steps to solve the Tableau.
    - ○ (a) Take the column with the highest negative number of the objective function.
    - ○ (b) Take the number within this column with the lowest ratio of T/number.
    - ○ (c) Set all numbers over and under the 4 to 0.
    - ○ (d) Divide all numbers right and left the 4 by 4.
    - ○ (e) Change the numbers in the green colored fields.
    - ○ (f) Repeat this procedure until no variable in the objective function is negative anymore.

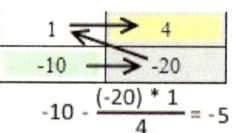

$$-10 - \frac{(-20) * 1}{4} = -5$$

- ○ **(5) Interpret your results.**

BV	x	y	Z_1	Z_2	Z_3	T
Z_1	0	0	1	-0.733	-4/3	120
x	1	0	0	0.133	-1/3	40
y	0	1	0	-0.033	1/3	60
OF	0	0	0	2/3	10/3	1600

=> Optimal quantities are x = 40 and y = 60 , profit is 1600.

- **(VI) Multi-Period Production Program Planning.**
  - Given information:
    - Total number of periods.
    - Demand forecasts for each period.
    - Production days each period.

Month	Demand	Cum. Demand	Prod. Days
Jan	900	900	22
Feb	1000	1900	18
Mar	1500	3400	21
Apr	1200	4600	21
May	800	5400	22
Jun	800	6200	20

  - **(1) Synchronization Strategy.**
    - Only produce the amount demanded.
    - Calculate the average demand per day: $\dfrac{demand}{production\ days} = \dfrac{900}{22} = 41$ and produce this amount.
  - **(2) Emancipation Strategy.**
    - Produce a constant amount each day and store the rest / take the missing amount from the storage.
    - Calculate average demand per day $= \dfrac{6200}{22 + 18 + \ldots + 22 + 20} = \dfrac{6200}{124} = 50$.
    - Calculate the periodic production $=$
      $average\ production * production\ days = 50 * 22 = 1100$.

- **(VII) ABC-Analysis.**
  - Given information:
    - Required units per period and unit costs.

Item	Annual usage	Unit costs
1	40,000	0.07
2	195,000	0.11
3	4,000	0.1
4	100,000	0.05
5	2,000	0.14
6	240,000	0.07
7	16,000	0.08
8	80,000	0.06
9	10,000	0.07
10	5,000	0.09

○ (1) Calculate the total periodic costs and rank them, starting with the highest value.

Item	1	2	3	4	5	6	7	8	9	10
Annual cost	2,800	21,450	400	5,000	280	16,800	1,280	4,800	700	450
Rank	5	1	9	3	10	2	6	4	7	8

○ (2) Calculate the percentage value of periodic costs of one product to total periodic costs.

Rank	1	2	3	4	5	6	7	8	9	10
Annual cost	21,450	16,800	5,000	4,800	2,800	1,280	700	450	400	280
%	39.8	31.1	9.3	8.8	5.2	2.4	1.3	0.8	0.8	0.5
Cum. %	39.8	70.9	80.2	89.0	94.2	96.6	97.9	98.7	99.5	100

○ (3) Set up a Lorenz-Curve to determine the goods.
  ▪ Determining 70 – 80% of the whole costs are A-goods.
  ▪ Determining less than 10% are C-goods.
    → Everything in between are B-goods.

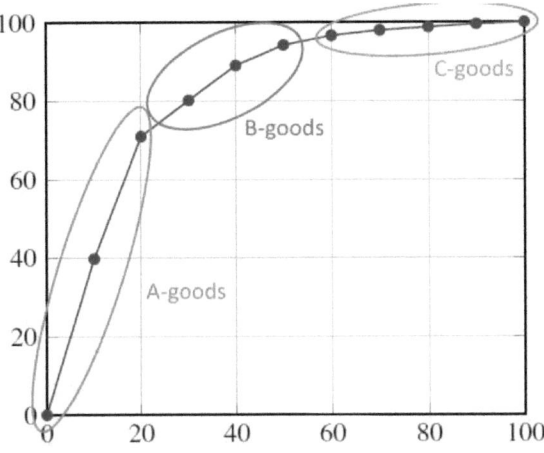

- **(VII) Safety Stock Calculation.**
  - *(1) Discrete Case.*
  - Given information: Demand during lead time (DDLT) and frequency of occurrence, service level (here 75%)

DDLT	2	3	4	5	6	7	8
Frequency	2	6	11	8	4	2	

- **(a) Determine the optimal order point.**
  - Sum up the total frequency and calculate the probability for each amount of DDLT.
  - When setting up the cumulative probability, search for a value close to service level and you've found your optimal ordering point.

Actual DDLT	Frequency	Probability	Cum. Probability
2	2	2/35	$2/35 \approx 0.0571$
3	6	6/35	$8/35 \approx 0.2286$
4	11	11/35	$19/35 \approx 0.5429$
5	8	8/35	$27/35 \approx 0.7714$
6	4	4/35	$31/35 \approx 0.8857$
7	2	2/35	$33/35 \approx 0.9439$
8	1	1/35	$34/35 \approx 0.9714$
9	1	1/35	$35/35 = 1$
	$\sum 35$		

- Colored area means: In more than 77% of all cases, the DDLT is 5 units or less, therefore optimal ordering point should be 5 units (call supplier for new delivery if inventory falls to 5 units; until the units are arrived, there is this "buffer" of 5 units).

39

z	.00
.0	.5000
.1	.5398
.2	.5793
.3	.6179
.4	.6554
.5	.6915
.6	.7257
.7	.7580
.8	.7881
.9	.8159
1.0	.8413
1.1	.8643
1.2	.8849
1.3	.9032
1.4	.9192
1.5	.9332
1.6	.9452
1.7	.9554
1.8	.9641
1.9	.9713
2.0	.9772

- **(b) Calculate the expected DDLT.**
  - Simply the weighted average of the table above
  - $EDDLT = 2*\dfrac{2}{35} + 3*\dfrac{6}{35} + 4*\dfrac{11}{35} + 5*\dfrac{8}{35}$.
  - $+ 6*\dfrac{4}{35} + 7*\dfrac{2}{35} + 8*\dfrac{1}{35} + 9*\dfrac{1}{35} = 4.6$
- **(c) Calculate the effective level of Safety Stock.**
  - The average amount of safety stock remaining in the inventory for more than 77% of all cases.
  - Strongly mathematical result, therefore calculate a percentage value.
  - $Safety\ Stock = s - EDDLT = 5 - 4.6 = 0.4$ Percentage value: $\dfrac{Safety\ Stock}{ordering\ point} = \dfrac{0.4}{5} =$ 8%.
- **(2) Safety Stock in continuous case.**
- Given information: mean demand (here: 693.7), standard deviation of demand (here: 139.27), service level (here: 95%).
  - Service level is value of our standardized "Quantil", therefore look at the tables for standardizes normal distribution and find the corresponding value for the service level (here: 1.6 or 1.7).
    - → In case of doubt: Always take the lower value (here: 1.6).
  - Now the standardization has to be undone, therefore use formula $s = mean + z * sigma$.
    - → $s = 693.7 + 1.6 * 139.27 = 916.532$
  - Optimal Safety Stock is simply $z * sigma$ $= 222.832$.

YOUR KNOWLEDGE HAS VALUE

- We will publish your bachelor's and
  master's thesis, essays and papers

- Your own eBook and book -
  sold worldwide in all relevant shops

- Earn money with each sale

Upload your text at www.GRIN.com
and publish for free